IKWUAZOM NNAMDI WENGA

Harmony Publishing
Plot 1 Emmanuel Anabor, Off Mopo Road, United Estate, Sangotedo,
Lagos, Nigeria
+2347032212481
publish@harmonypublishing.com.ng

ISBN: 9781005505707

Book cover design by Shobola IbukunOluwa

Book layout by Eswari Kamireddy

Printed in Nigeria.

Dedication

This book is dedicated to God almighty, the giver of life and wisdom. I also dedicate it to my mother; she's been my strongest supporter. To aunty AU Nzegwu and her children: Nneka, Chike, Nonso and Tochukwu, may God never cease to bless you all. Also, I dedicate this book to Loveth Amarachi, Shedracks Joy Adaora, Chinwe Ebo, Iveanyi Nezianya and Nwando Ogbuotobo.

I specially dedicate this book also to the people of Palestine and Gaza. May God see you through this nightmare.

Finally, to the victims of rape, police brutality, depression, suicide, cultural discrimination and child abuse, this book is dedicated to us all. May you never lose hope and light in the darkness of this world.

Foreword

Nnamdi Patrick Wenga is a new voice from the great nation of Nigeria, poised to brave the path once traveled by some of the compatriots before them.

Thankfully, the literary landscape is big and fertile enough for many that dare to profess their love affair with their muse for the reading and enjoyment of the world.

Nnamdi's debut collection of poems titled *Heartbeats by the River*, is a literary gem with poems like 'Warm", where the persona tells us "I'm the sun that melts the glacier" and still wonders "Do my eyes summon the gods"?

In "My Country", the patriot in Wenga shines through, where he takes responsibility for whatever he makes his country out to be. Bravely and with pride, he beats his chest to say, "This is my birth and death; bloody nights, still in it I shine". Also, in his poem "Nigeria", he exalts the beauty in diversity, likening its physical beauty to that of "Eden".

Wenga ararticulates his sensuality and he gets "lost in my feelings" and through this poem like his other romantic poems "Amazon Queen", " Crazy, Wild Romance", etc, he appreciates the beauty and queenliness, hopefully, of the African woman, but then love knows no colour.

Solace can one find in poetry for on another day poets could be preachers of peace. Wenga's "Resilience comes from within" preach that though sometimes, we find ourselves swinging between spaces, we are more than the trials we face.

These themes and many more perfectly run through the collection with a touch of poetic exaltation. With a poet like Wenga, it's certain that there would be many more from where these came from.

Samuella Julia Conteh,
Order of Shakespeare medalist,

Author of _Love Colours_ and _The Unsung Song_

Love has Colours

Sinful Maiden

A song for my sins,
But yet no music.
My loins in conflict with my soul,
A soul long lost to lust
I crave for Hades and bliss in heaven
I beg for a ride unto cries in pleasure
My body acts on a solo drive
Making me teary downtown
She would love to moan your name,
Don't ask me who, me?
Nights have I gone to bed soaked from your smiles
Let me wet your face and make your beards drip
Lemme shudder and vibe in throes on you.
Make me cry and yet wrap you till you're clawed up
Chastise my lust into deeper valleys
But wait, damn, yet another dreamy night

Lost in my feelings

I know of a certain beautiful maiden
Who bears the loveliest smile
And her steps certainly worthy of a queen
In her eyes are the keys to heaven hidden.

She's simple yet she exudes elegance so rare
With as much as a touch does she send sweet shivers
Down the spines of love-struck warriors
Taming even the bravest to lilly hearted babies.

The sounds of her laughter reverberate in the halls
of my soul
Drawing emotions so deeply rooted from my soul
I'm lost in awe at the aura of her beauty
For she only needs to breathe for the stars to bow.

Dreams of her spectacular skin adorn my mind
For how can one be so flawless and still be human
I wonder what her touch would feel like
Definitely it must be as soft as the wools of Persia.

Feelings birthed by my sincere admiration and desire
To feel and hold her close in my arms close to my heart
Clouds my head and blurs my planned perfect speeches
Making a word smith like me lose my words hopelessly.

HEARTBEATS BY THE RIVER

She's the lady my heart yearns for
The fire that burns against the gushing winds
But allow me be and disturb me not for somewhere deep inside
I'm with my maiden and lost in my feelings.

(To the one with the sweetest smiles)

Amazon Queen

Standing tall over the skies
With a stern but milky gaze
A soul so pure the gods wonder
Her smile blowing off the mountains
Her heart still remains unexplored
For her love never ends
Eyes as though they were stars
Steps like a dove but as sure as a lioness
In her beauty found a home
With her have the ancients found reincarnation,
For she is old in wisdom but young in beauty
Ageless daughter of her fathers and clans
Teach us to smile, and live your legend
For in you have the heavens birthed a queen

wildfires

Like wildfire did they begin,
Spreading fast and sure
Her charm was her pureness
His strength lay in his quest for truism
Under the sun did their love shine
The moon playing them tunes of cupid
Even the stars got jealous and happy
So the gods cursed them
To be happy forever without tears

Songs on the Blue World

To songs heart and soul sway
More songs by the blue waters
Staring up the blue heavens

The dark knight prince and his moonlight
She was and is and would always be
The muse of the ancients
Hold my hands, dear sun,
For under the moon shall lovers moan
In tune to melodies thought gone
But now risen

Clouds

Look me in the eyes
And tell him she loves me
Draw circles round my nose
Tickle his wings and seduce her fire
Let judge & jury dance in jail,
For feathers inspire my weight
She smiles like his lover,
And he flows like her oceans
Paddle let's go they say to us
He nods at her and hugs his lover
The muse of the befallen in bliss
Lies in the nothingness of fear
I found her in her
And she laid claim to his soul
Now they rule our clouds
For out of nothing but hearted pain
Did they find endless love
Deep is deeper when deep enough

Resurrection

A thousand haughty words we say
Will always bow to the love we share
As the fire burns and ashes gather
Only then is our Phoenix unveiled
The air have we given hope
Fires have we tamed to tender
The waters ever swaying to our rhythm
And the sands in eternal loyalty
Hold me as you
For the sails have just been set
Kill my fears and inner deaths
For I'll murder your past demons
Look us in our eyes and swear to sanity
That I didn't steal your heart,
And you didn't rob me of my soul
Only then shall we die in living

Fallacy

I trusted but only to fallacy
I rose but only to fall deeper
Trust ye no heart
And bond not with mortal souls
For they look not beyond mere words
Promises seeming like banter to some
Trust is ever doubt to them
Boasts of valor and forever standing,
But yet at the moments of truism
Those feet heartbreakingly did flee
Life is stringent to moments
Love is life only if breaths remains

To the Lady like her

Keeper of his soul
Founder of their path
Muse of his musings
To her did he submit
And to her rhythm
Does he dance and sway
Request not his heart
For you have paid in full
With the grandest of means
He loves you beyond this life
You own his every smile

I Stand

I stand on our thousand feet
As we walk towards our tomorrow
Loving you in new ancient ways
Our souls ever becoming one

Heart and Soul

Like the august rains you came,
Ever steady and intentional.
Like fire did you burn Drawing me deep unto rays
That rival and groom the sun.
To a lamb have you turned my lion.
To roses have my vain steel returned.
I have lived and loved this love and life,
But ever hearing not the tears of bliss.
Sooth my inner and fuel my galaxy,
The moon bears witness to this,
For under her did we bloom and smile
My heart melts my ribs.
I have found my sunshine in your submission.
In your smiles have I found my voice.
In those eyes do the future beckon.
Never have my feet found more grace in steps.
This tango of our souls will never end.
Hold my inner and lead me to your days.
That we may dazzle through my nights.
In that big little world of ours,
Created and guarded by our souls.

Roads of despair

Our lonely roads of despair,
Led us both down to this point.
Our tears and pain in seeking air,
Found the wind even better.
My wings ever growing and full.
Your oceans rising above the seas.

In your silence I found my voice.
In your night I found dawn.
From my ashes did your Phoenix arise.
In your love did I berth to anchor.
My eyes glow to your dreams.
May we never be woken.

The storms surely will gather.
The rains may still yet cease.
The earth may even turn barren.
But we have the stars to smile at us.
The moon will play sweet tunes.
And the sun shall brighten our souls.

Feel my footsteps upon your heart.
Sing to my unheard sanity.
Dance to the tunes I lost.
Lemme watch you whisper your echoes.
Why don't you just leap into my soul,

And definitely do us a tango.

We're in love today beginning tomorrow.
I love you always since yesterday.
I will love your darkest of lights.
I'll embrace your fears into trust and hope.
I'll squeeze and trouble you in bliss,
For we're you and I forever

Tesoro

A stream of beauty and grace.
A fountain of life and love.
By your side have I found myself
In you does my inner dwell
With you shall I reign.
The past though haughty and dark
Have our love subdued.
Our tears, fears and doubts,
Have we turned to gold,
Selling only unto ourselves.
My empress and muse,
My sunshine and moonlight,
Forever a future are we.
Listen, for my heart whispers.
In languages crafted by us.
Listen, for my soul sings.
To tunes and beats of our musing.
Dance then and giggle my woman,
For long have we been in denial,
In a world lacking of purity and life.
Dear soul keeper of times and love,
Hold my inner and lead me to light.
Dreams of our souls do we share.
Laughter and smiles ever entwined.
Listen, my night beholds your day.
In your submission do I thrill,

O thrills of our knowing.
Hold me as we sway and tango,
Into our very own world.

Amore

My lady *amore mio*
My love at first sight
My ever-undying love
My sunshine and rainbow
In you have I berthed
With you have I set sail
Together shall we endlessly loot
From the spoils of bliss and love
Tesoro of my seasons
You have grasped to never release
My unclean poor spirit and soul
With nothing but pure innocence
And a shared pen bound in musings
I hail thee my fair damsel.

song bird

I shall sing a song
But only when the night
Has put the doves to sleep
And the owls are free
To pay the bats a visit

Let's Dance again tonight

My past,
Hurt, heartbreaks, lies,
Tears, promises broken and
a soul battered beyond repair.

My fears,
loving too much, needing so much,
Caring for the wrong people
and getting dropped just so close.

My heart can barely take anymore,
My inner sanctum torn to shreds.
The taste of true love now so bitter,
More or less a distant old relish.

Then just about when the curtains fall,
She waltzes in, taking the air hostage adorably.
Seducing the sun with her grace and kissing the moon.
A true definition of divinity and class personified.

My heart skips in awe and my lips bow.
For once I smile with no reason but for reality.
My past comes creeping behind my fears and for once,
I slap off the old me and take a step forward.

Hands stretched out for a dance.

I look into her eyes and I lose my doubts,
My hands grab and pull her closer, she smells like roses.
Our hearts pounding and racing with the unknown.

Fears, doubts, our souls seek and weigh in.
It seems all like a dream, dreams we wish lasts forever.
In her arms I find safety, comfort and peace.
For her smiles promise a future without judgment.

I see her fears through those searching eyes.
I feel her passion for this new found fires in our hearts.
I know she seeks answers, but fears the same fate,
The one her love has cursed her with.

But we take this leap into the blues waters,
Bare to beautiful charming skins, eyes locked
And soul gazing, our bonds getting bolder by
each breathe.
Come my berry, let's dance our souls into love tonight.

When The Earth Comes Swords Drawn

For ages have we maligned nature
Milking her to dizziness
Taking her mildness as weakness
Cutting her trees and polluting her seas.
Hunting down her forest children
We're the villains in this race
Turning the world shattered
In the wake of our greed and reckless behavior.
Now nature has had enough and has vowed revenge
By increasing the heat, drying the waters had
And by flooding us has she struck her severe blows
We're no match against her wrath
For she has endured long enough
Hoping we may change our ways
All she needed was love and appreciation,
something that this generation has found impossible to render
But how do we appease her?
How do we soothe her pain?
Only by truly showing remorse
By planting ten trees for each fallen
By planting shrubs to beautify her skin
By stopping pollution and all
By protecting the wildlife and their habitats

By being conscious if the atmosphere and
Our environment in all we do and do not do
Only when we've shown sincerity in our repentance,
Shall nature turn the world for us in peace
Only then shall the climates and favor us.
Until then we're slaves unto our ignorance.

Love Vibes

Like early morning dews
Your beauty wets my heart
Like the holiest of Jews
Shall my faith know no doubt

In you have I found feet
Bringing me ever close to perfection
The taste of your lips so sweet
That I dance in anticipation

Your eyes as piercing as bullets
But yet as assuring as soul promises
Your skin glowing like golden bracelets
As you waltz into my premises

In your arms do I find love again
For your heart knows no lie
Hold me close yet again
With wings out that we may fly

Love Shall Come

Love shall come in the after thought
Love shall come when you've lost hope
Love shall come in the nights of loneliness
Love shall come in the mornings of self-doubt
Love shall come when all hopes are faded
Love will brighten your gloomy stars
And wash clean your stained heart
Love shall prove your soul worthy of love
Love would pat your heart assuredly and
Whisper strength unto your frail soul
You're going to feel this love someday
Just when before the curtains fall
For your love itself untamed and dauntless
Aiming for the skies with nothing but love

My woman, my muse

Death is never the song of the angels
Yet you killed my fears and doused my flame,
Bringing me unto a higher place of warmth.
Armed with nothing but a true and homely heart,
And a smile that beats my imagination of heaven.
In your soul has my love anchored in peace.
Your laughter ever bringing me to joyful whisperings,
For I ask myself if I am deserving of your grace.
So young this love maybe but how right it feels,
As though an heir to an ancient throne.
The days turn to nights and seasons peep,
All in a rush to usher in forever.
My lady of youth and joyful heartbeats,
A story one day shall be told to ears and nature
Of a lady who ruled and owned his heart,
And her soul finder who was undeserving but chosen.
May their morning find the wisdom of the ancient times
And their nights the fluidity of the quiet oceans.

****Crazy Wild Romance****

Like floating clouds
My fingers roam your body
Each touch drawing satisfactory gasps
I feel your skin yearn for more
Your hairs woken in attention
Our gazes lock as I lift your head
Running my fingers against your temple
As I lean in for a kiss
Your hands find my head and pull me lower
Our tongues engaging in fierce sweet combat
My hands find your breasts I twitch your nipples
I smile into our kiss as your body stiffens
I feel your grip get stronger and needy
I caress and fondle your breast steadfastly
Kneading them like my mother kneads dough
Little moans escape your busy lips
I take my tease lower, drawing imaginary lines
Till I find your gates unto bliss
I'm greeted by your wetness, dripping and teary
My fingers dance around your clit
Making little brushes here and there
You jerk and moan my name faintly
Now I disengage our lips to your obvious dismay
I kiss my way down your neck
Each touch earning moans louder by the count
My lips seduce your nipples to attention

I feel you shiver and gasp, cursing adorably
As I go to town on your nipples
Sucking on them like my life depends on it
Your moaning intensifies and you grab unto my head
Pulling me ever closer and begging
My fingers now invade your juicy box
In inspirational pace and precision
You can bear no more and so you scream out
Your body stiffens and you convulse and jerk
as you whore into the throes of orgasms

Will you be here

Good times are like water, everywhere,
but yet the desert dwells without the luxury.
the throes of ecstasy can only last moments.
even the sun in all its harsh splendor,
has the moon to contend with for dominance.

We've seen the good and many bad times.
you've sprinkled upon me the waters of love,
when my heart was burning with sadness.
you have nursed my damaged inner sanctum,
ever reassuring me of your undying loyalty and love.

Together we've been soil and grape alike,
producing wine only the masters of old romance
could comprehend enough to dare consume.
in you I found true peace and pristine love.
a jewel so old and yet so modern.

But will you be here when the sun sets?
will you still jump on me like a leopard?
will I still be your heart and fire?
will I still be your day and darkness as raw?
each passing day sketches winds on my garden.

But I'll be here till tomorrow and forever
loving you in ways befitting a goddess

singing you songs by the lake on our love boat
sweeping you off your feet till we pass out tired
and till breath flies away, we'll be here.

Morning nectar

Windows opening unto the morning rays
The remnants of the night creeping away.
The birds seem to agree to a need to sing
So they render their soul lifting melodies
To an appreciating audience... Yes audience
I lean down and kiss her forehead
Starting the ritual of waking my sun to my eyes
She mutters gibberish and stirs around adorably
I have never seen a sight more beautiful
I kiss her lips this time caressing her cheeks
She smiles in her dreams and calls my name
Have you been lucky to see a morning star?
I drop lower and cuddle her up, feeling her lips
Her eyes... Oh those eyes open up my soul
She wakes with a smile, one that spells paradise
My heartbeat right here in my arms, my heart flutters.
She cuddles back and gives me that loving squeeze
She smiles and draws me down on her
I feign struggling to get up but only wanting more
She looks into my eyes and drops a kiss
I decide when we rise to the morning
And with that the blanket takes the stage

Ecstasy

Hold me my dear
Pin me down to your bed
Stripping me ever so assuringly
Till only my soul is cladded
Fingers drapping down my cheeks
I feel your breath down my neck
Whispering sweet evil into my senses
Seducing my sanity unto blissful flaws
Schooling my lust to greater heights
Fanning my flames of want
Take me and make me beg
Squash my mounds of milky nectar
Till my breath ceases Tickle down my spine and ribs
Move your tongue ever precisely
Mentor my snack box on salsa and tango
Squeeze my little bell of a clit
Till she weeps to the deaf world
While you steadfastly lap up her floods
Make me scream your name
I wanna curse you so sweetly
I wanna drown you in my fluids
Bite marks adorn your neck
And my nails decorate your back
Blackout...convulsions embrace
Sending shivers down my spine
I lovingly strangle you in vain luck

My inner speaking in the unknown
Singing your adulations and tribute
Ruthless vibes and thrills sway my limbs
As my orgasms shatter my morality

***** *love unworthy* ***

Like the early morning dews wet my feet,
your thoughts moisturize my soul
bringing my heart unto deeper climes of emotions.
your eyes as piercing as golden bullets,
but only piercing this time through my fears and doubts.

My hurting heart bleats of hurt and neglect,
but in your voice do I hear sanity and peace,
in your touch does my inner sanctum find comfort,
Scraping away years of emotions gone sour and bitter.
my body, heart and soul I dance to you.

Your steps remind me of the ancient moons and queens,
for you make grace and divinity seem so easy to bear.
I see the sun smile at you and I know the moon
has always
nursed feelings for you, the stars ever jealous of your aura.
bless my hearts and water my fountain of love.

Your hands in mine feel like destiny,
for I feel we've loved this morning in our yesterdays.
but only if I truly believed in reincarnation of hearts.
I know the days of inner fights may come, but I
take each step
unto loving you in the spirit of true love.

** *friendship unknown* **

We merely stumbled upon each other
our hellos and chats ever so simple
Her smile blowing my feet away
her eyes held truths so pure and untamed
her soul ever trying to resurrect the feelings lost
but her heart bore a grudge; against the angels unknown
and by so swearing affinity to the demons at hand.

My mind feels her pain, for I'm pain personified
built to sinful perfection and bound for the re-
turn journey
in my heart are my fears hidden and knighted
but yet my pen spares no villain nor demon
singing monsters into angels through my outpours
I feel her teary soul and I reach out in fraternal flames
but her doubts are as holy as the fallen angels.

She feels this life, but dreads this life
over and yet again has she loved un sparingly
but only to have her fragmented heartbroken more
She's only human and so I judge not her rejection of love
for she has seen the throes of bliss turned to sorrow
and has sworn to embrace her hurt and shut her doors
yet her soul cries out from behind those doors,
but helpless.

HEARTBEATS BY THE RIVER

Our fires find energy so rare and precise
for two can love if one is willing
my doubts ever manly and unbending, her fears
bearing seeds
her lips have lost the taste of truthful kisses
her hips ever shying away from swaying to my
sincere touch
her voice would I love to sing my name in adulation
as I carry her inner sanctum unto higher realms.

But yet we bond, getting stronger each day
building walls around our darkness shared
caressing our souls and melting our pains into jewels
Looking forward to each passing wind and moonlight
my heart skips at the thought of her graceful steps
as she waltzes into my senses, my smiles gaining weight
she's my unknown friend from the blue free world.

***** *Whispers for my lover* *

In those lonely moments,
When the pains of heartbreaks past
Come crashing down on my heart,
You're the reason for those comforting smiles.
You're the hose that sprinkles my garden of love.
In you have I found complete peace.
By your side do I find my steps.
Your words lift up my pulse and my ears crave for
your voice.
My fingers feel empty without yours intertwined
with them.
You've brought life back upon my long dead heart.
Your love showers my heart with undeserving love
and passion.
In your eyes are the biggest jewels hidden, open only to
my knowing eyes.
My arms beg to hold you again,
My eyes speak in loud whispers my passion and undy-
ing loyalty.
Dreams of forever dance across my heart.
The future seems so far but yet so close my love.
Today with you would be my best but tomorrow longer is
my prayer.

****They're Only but Wishes ****

This night came not like any other.
Even the stars seemed as though on an errand.
my body craving and starving, of your care.
I try to imagine you close to me, but lust dims my head.
I rub my thighs against the other, seeking damn-
ing friction.
The air feels so hot suddenly despite the vents.
My manicured fingers roam absentmindedly,
dwelling finally to tweak my heaving nipples.
Goosebumps run across my body, making me shudder.
My thighs aggressively find moisture and a rhythm.
I can still feel your breath down my neck as
you whispered
the blissful torture you'd love to subject me to.
I can still feel your palms cupping my breasts to attention,
Breathtaking moans softly screaming in my head.
"I'll take you when you're ready" those were your words.
I would have sworn you would tear my clothes to shreds,
Judging from the lust in your eyes, but no you left.
Leaving me in this state of insane drives and lust.
I can smell my musky scent by the minute, shit!
I'm going so crazy and my waists rolls without control,
As though you were piling into me. I can't bear anymore.
I slip one hand down into my crotch and a moan escapes.
I rub on my bell furiously and with two fingers
slipping in,

I go to town on my juice box, my legs vibing and shaking.
I feel that familiar feeling as my toes curl up in ecstasy.
My body shudders and I scream my ascension out,
Damn, did my fingers feel as though dipped in oil.
And gradually I returned to sanity... but only waking
to find my fingers in my cunny and soaked like hell.
Do dreams come any better?

Gratitude to a lover.

My fire and love...
Like the august rain you came, ever expected.
My words for you are already known to your heart.
You've brought so much happiness and calm in just
little time
Thanks for being a life jacket when the river over flooded
the banks.
You're surely loved.

Runway Goddess.

Like a goddess on a runway, she awes all.
Her beauty melting seamlessly into our hearts.
Her radiant glow blinds the vain sun.
Daughter of her fathers, dame of the night.
Her eyes are windows into the future,
For deep in them do we see & seek peace.
With a body built to perfection,
A heart tended to by the heavens,
Her soul watered only by unknown bliss.
From her smiles do the gods speak.
A body befitting only but divinity,
With hips carved to dropping perfection.
Hail lady, bless us with your touch.
You're beautiful beyond words,
And your seasons without end.

**Love Intense*

Rare
Bold
Loving
Adorable
Charming....

Once upon a peek,
Another peek,
Messages, laughter...
And now a love story....
Ndo nwa, the jewel from ogbeodogwu anike, you have tamed the lion and frozen the volcano......
To love and more...

Kambili

Dear daughter of mine born queen
A jewel of old now born to our generation
My most precious jewel unrivaled
Your love compared only with your mother
I'll sing you lullabies to sleep
I'll cuddle you while I sing your praises
I'll sing my heart out to the heavens for you
In your eyes I see starts and moons dancing
In your giggles do I see the sun hidden in bliss
One day you'll drag my hair and tug hard
You'll pinch my nose and smile
Surely you would make me chase you around
I know must the right games we could play together
We'll make your mother so jealous and green
I'll carry you up on my shoulders and feel you tense
Your first steps would last in my soul forever
That took in your eyes as you took on the world
I wish I could understand why you cried most times
But I need you to know 'm here forever
To love you and to cherish you till that moment
When breathe and motion fails to stay
I'll read you stories by your bedside
And take you fishing by he take and cheering
you onto your first catch
We'll gossip about mom and boys
I'll teach you kindness and humility

I'll show you how to care for others and
I'll show you how to treat nature and her seeds
Life with you will be awesome and lovely
Watching you fall asleep and covering you up
My pain seeing you off to college a grown woman
Trying to assure myself that the world needs you
maybe more than i do need you
I know one day you'll bring him home
and tell me he's the one I've always dreaded
The one who would steal you away from me
And then your day comes to my blissful nightmare
I'll give my love away to a man forever
Tears form in my eyes and as I look across
To your mother as she smiles amidst her tears
Walking you down the aisle is the hardest duty
For a father who truly gave his all to his duty
As i watch you both share that kiss
It dawns on me that you're gone for good
And that your happiness is supreme
I'll still recount our stories in my mind and smile
For no matter where you go my baby
You'll always remain my Kambili

**lost faiths.*

My fathers were the originals.
They saw the world for what it was.
They communed with their ancestors.
They revered the spirits of the dead.
Building bonds stronger than life itself.
My fathers had name for all the stars, even for the moon.
The sun was worshipped and revered.
Early morning incantations were offered
to please their ancestors, spirits and gods.
They believed in unity and devotion.
Everything had a reason and a place in their destiny.
Each child born was named according to his sup-
posed stars.
But now we've lost touch with our past.
All in the search for civilization.
My generation has derailed from the roots of our very
existence.
We have lost the faith to fate.
A lost faith indeed.

whispers and random thrills

Warm

The wind blows and
The drummer redeems his steps
I'm the sun that melts the glacier
Looking up the stars,
Do my eyes summon the gods?

Spotted

Even in the dark, we are still spotted
Like wolves roaming the gardens.
My butterflies perch up the mountains
These flows are music unto my strings,
Drawing the stars towards the sun.
Tell me you hear my heartbeats,
And I'll show you our fire
In our tomorrow are our echoes buried,
Be my snowy flame

Mystery

Deep up the mountain
Do I find blue waters
Salty rivers purified by the clouds
Eagles now fed to the chickens
Fires bowing to the Phoenix
For we await the moon at dawn

Waterfalls

In the clouds way up above,
Do I light my fires of wisdom
In slow royal steps, have I seen a dance
As slippery eels and slimy mucus,
So are my words unreachable
For I speak a language still unborn
Waterfalls replace tears unheard
For my soul looms aloof
My heart as heavy as feathers
My inner sanctum finds yet no priest
I beg to berth this ship of slander
Let he who finds meaning to insanity
Help me walk this voice

vain lusts

I can't be the good friend you crave
I am not even close to being nice
I am everything vile and ugly
I am mean and hard
I might never even change
You always detest my arrogance
But wait
My ego derails such humor
You forever crave my touch
My whispers drive you insane
My obelisk eternally bereaving your juice box
Thus she wets and sheds sweet tears of bliss -
You'll never stop needing me.
But wait
Why beg for my fidelity and loyalty?
When you know I am ever a ranger
I please and tease all that share the lust
I am your joy and gloom in abstraction
Gifting you orgasms as I please and will.
I remain a god over your intimates and lust.

Freestyle

The life of a poet
Is not to sip Moet.
Dreams of living cozy
Lure me from being lazy
Like meows of a cat
The lines pair with your heart
And like a purring kitten
Your heart is love stricken
As must goats retire to their pen,
So must I rest my pen.

Loafer

She called me a loafer.
She said I was too bad.
She said I was a whore.
She said I was anything but faithful.
But I said wait, my dear,
You see this my tongue,
You see these my fingers,
And you see my soldier
They are members of a brotherhood,
And should they unite to meet you
You'll sing the songs that will melt you
Only then shall you know,
That I am a loafer with skills like no other.

Life is stringent

Life is stringent to moments
Life is morning unto the stars.
Life is sunset to our struggles.
Life is the muse and fire,
The pot that cooks the lions heart.
Life is nothing but dust
Hold unto nothing in life, yet glue unto life.
Bliss in living and soulful in thought.
Is life without and with life.

I Love You

I love you, I do
I love you, dear friend
I love you, oh mother
I love you, dear father
I love you, my country
I love you clan and kindred spirits all
I love you more than I did yesterday
But lesser than I would tomorrow.

Blissful Fallacy

On upward hills down below
Does the river flow.
Seducing the heavens in all splendor.
Many have searched in futility,
For its source Don't we commit t to fallacy
Of rivers flowing upwards?

Silence

Silence is often loud and heavy
Patience ever boring and drunk.
Faith decided by some fate.
Pins fall and the ground shakes.
When did feathers add some pounds more?
Fish have grown legs on sand.
These mysteries may never end,
Until they find bearing in our phoenix.

flamingo

Beautiful slender fortress
Of dazzling beauty and grace
Armed with pure elegance
On long enchanting legs
That stoop to bless the waters

snow

White frozen stone drops everywhere
Forming icy mountains
And making my bones jittery
Like a bowl of jelly
Which never falls

Rains

It starts as little drops Slowly washing the grounds
Nothing too dirty to withstand
The bath and purge of nature
Ever steady and ever cleansing

Grace of the fallen

I wake up today not forgetting yesterday
My stomach tightened and my jaws raving
Hunger fills the air like some cheap cologne
Rabid rats scurry off at my noisy yawning
What good neighbors we have become
Feeding and stealing off each other's stashes, if any.

I manage to get hold of some faint aroma
It must be my head playing games with me
For who in these slums we call home and abode
Can afford such heavenly allure without being murdered
By wolfish hungry neighbors in a second
It all seems strange but tempting.

Outside my stall the aroma gets bolder
And then I hear the drums and chants
I still can't see the people behind such light
Then I hear the masquerade cries and I jitter
It must be the festival we've seen occasionally
But this time with the smell of food.

I leap with my last energy in joy
The devil has remembered me today
My heart breaths solace to my aching legs
And I set my gaze up the heavens in awe
And wonder how gracious the devil comes
Truly he must be an angel.

**Beautiful rains*

The clouds gather in obvious dialogue,
As though they were in session.
The wind blows ever assuredly, seducing the trees
into a dance.
The birds fly in frenzy for they know the signs.
The chickens gather their chicks and march home in a
delectable convoy.
Mothers screaming out to their kids to come inside, and
the children in deliberate deafness continue their playing.
The weather needs no soothsayer.
The first drops arrive and then like a purging river,
The sky sends her gift down; sweet rain.
Long have we waited and the heat long
Unbearable, but now the rain is here.
Slapping on roof tops and washing man
And nature to sparkling Purity.

the local flavour

My Country

This is my country
My home and pride
This is my birth and death
Bloody nights still, in it I shine
My land of war and pride
This time is none other
The generation of the lost angels
Finally has seen the light

Nigeria

A great land you are
Standing in unified diversity
Your flock ever so beautiful
You feed all in nature
And from your godly waters
You quench their thirst
From the northern Sahel and deserts,
To the Southern creeks and swamps,
To the western forests and seas
Down to the eastern farms and rivers
All speak of your rare divinity
Your beauty ever matchless
Eden you must be
Mother of all roots
Cradle of our existence
All hail Nigeria

**Onicha Ado* (my home and identity)*

Gifting us ancestors worthy of our libations
Spirit The morning star of the eastern cape
The beauty by the waters
History as old as the ancients
Purified royalty laced in grandeur
Lord of the southern sun

Bearer of legends and myth
Abode of the gods themselves
A city fortified by mystery and wonder
The bowel that holds humanity in diversity
A tower of splendor and accomplishment

A god king on the throne
A mortal immortal born human
Stronger than all but one of all
To him do the spirits sing to
Fanning his reign with humility

Posterity pays homage to your name
For your sons and daughters glow unhindered
Exporting your glory to the world and beyond
uality of the purest form indeed

A culture so unique in all ramifications
Masquerades beautiful to mortal envy
Dances so godly they make the heavens smile
The royal drums blessing the universe with rarity
This land must be the Eden of old born new

Her maidens as radiant as the roman sun
Their beauty demystifying the queens of old
Her sons built to dropping masculinity
Conquerors of yesterday and forever
A breed so rare and pristine

A land bonded in unity of heritage
The land of spirits, gods, myth and humility
Abode of wisdom, love and peace
You're the reason the sun shines forever
onicha ado n'idu, the land of possibilities.

Ogbuefi

I watch in awe and wonder
As my papa prepares his apparel
He moves with acute precision
Setting each piece as though a divine purpose
Well that's what he embodies I guess
For he mediates between us and our souls gone
A pristine confluence of the living and the dead
Mama says he is a priest of sorts
I always wondered what the white apparel meant
Until he led me into his iba and explained.
Out of angelic joy and newfound appreciation
I ran off to brag to my peers that my ancestors
Lived with us in our iba and that papa fed them daily
The looks of genuine amazement on their faces
Made me adore papa to new heights
I was drawn back to reality by mama's salutations
"Ogbuefi," she called out in adoration.
Yes, that's my papa.

Local

You call me local because I speak my tongue.
You who is born of my very same roots.
A little hangout with foreign books and tales,
Have suddenly made you different
Now the mud seems dirty to you.
I spit on your first cries unto nature

Now your culture is just some study and thesis.
The lands that you waltzed on now sites for leisure.
Your oracles you now see as artifacts and tales,
Merely told for fun by craggy old dirty locals
How do you sleep at night? When you remember,
That those dirty fingers bathed and fed you.

I know your name and we were clan brothers.
Your ancestors were high chiefs and warriors.
Now you wear fancy robes and smoke long pipes,
And that shitting bowl you call a hat
Drink from the ovaries of nature and
See if she wouldn't have you dead

You call my food poisoning and you mock my markings.
Isn't that hypocritical of you knowing you bear same?
But let me tell you, no matter how foreign you
Have become, you remain a local to the galaxies,
And lifetimes to come unending, you are and shall
Always be a foreign local boy.

Homely Rivers

No quiet day still yet
Inpatient drivers hurling insults like gifts
Intriguing madness and pure sophistication
I'm one of many who have lived with this luxury
A little banter here and there wouldn't hurt
So I set my cycle down and watch the traffic
They say the city is wild and dirty and mean
But to me it remains my sanctuary of gold
Instead of filth, I see a city equal to old Egypt
A city thriving in underestimated myths
There's something you feel here that melts elsewhere
The soul of resilience and fortitude
I've heard talks of the city by the blue waters,
being a better life teacher, but the truth remains
That my city by the brown waters has no rival
For the ocean has no playmate within
Oh my city, land of homely rivers.

*******Africanism is a soul*******

The faces of crying poor children
doesn't portray you. The tales of poverty,
war and ignorance explain you not.
Centuries of mutilation, exploitation
and racism have still not dampened
the fire of your spirit. Tales of your
riches and splendor, will forever attract fantasies.
You lie not in the many rivers that abound in you.
Your color and heritage goes beyond being black.
You're cradle of civilization, the bed of
mysticism and ancient valor. Your seeds have for
ages overcome and conquered all obstacles.
You hold not unto the scars of your hurt
nor the memories of your pain.

Let not the world in obvious alliance
with vain wisdom, make you feel less
of who you are. For the piercings, tattoos,
markings, folklores, music, dance, dressings,
languages and gods of your seeds are forever
voices and colors of redemption.
In the chants and echoes of nature
have you found your feet, taking steps
so gracious the heavens marvel.
You lie not in mere flesh nor bones,
You're anchored to never depart, only in

the deepest and warmest of places.
You're Africa and you have lived forever,
beyond maps, tales and people.
You live in the very souls of your seeds....

#This piece is dedicated to all victims of moral sentiments, racism and cultural segregation. We're Africa and not just black people...

flamingo

Beautiful slender fortress
Of dazzling beauty and grace
Armed with pure elegance
On long enchanting legs
That stoop to bless the waters

life, hope, immortality and musings

(Laughter)

An amazing feeling, finding passage,
From my heart to my lips.
Blessing the atmosphere in sweet seducing sounds.
Call it joy or happiness if you choose.
Its more than that but all of that for me.
It's my perception of gratitude to my heart,
For by those heart melting bliss of sounds,
I pour out all my troubles, worries and thanks.
It's not just beautiful, it is wonderful and alluring.
I laugh my soul into deeper musing and fire,
Drawing energy from the smiles on your faces,
As you try holding back your laughter.
Happiness is free and so is love.
The only thing we ever have to work for is pain.
For by shutting out our hearts upon love, joy and peace,
What more is there to expect if not pain.
Laugh with me and join me as I gaze deeper into peace.

Inner Musings

Open my mind to you
Take my soul unto you
Chastise my lust into trust
That my heart may never rust
Tip the lamp of vanity
That the beam of truism may invade
Hold my inner and lead me in wonder
For long without grip have I wandered
Hope is a rhythm too costly for the soulless
Fugitive have I turned my conscience into
Taking my 'man' away from the man
Some roses too thorny to love
Yet some bullets ever so assuring
As though piercing my pain
This heart knows no bounds over here
Yet it remains bound by denials
Looking gloomy as though a puppy starved
But the ink runs dry brethren
And so I must bow to unearth
This inner muse must I breed

It's Okay

The world may never get to know me
The stars may never align in my favor
The sun may deny me light in my darkness
The moon may deny my night glow
But it's only for a moment. It's okay.

The heavens may shut its doors on my cries
Fate may determine my faith or otherwise
Family and friends may become like the enemy
The holy robes may ever castigate my immorality
This too shall pass. It's okay.

When my smiles lack sincerity, I hope you still smile
despite that
My condolences to my days of peace and laughter
These days seem in rivalry with hope and light
And everything around me becomes toxic
But like the winds, this shall pass. It's okay.

I watch the birds in awe as they go about blessing the skies
I feel the grass on my bare feet and wonder at
their comfort
I envy the rivers as I run my fingers through it,
such fluidity
Nature really has no rival except the creator in beauty

I draw in the calming scents of the lilies and my
soul melts.

On days like this, all I promise myself is stability
The strength to stay focused and the will to survive
I know better days have been and still will come
abundantly
I know the dead can't do better and so I must live to fight
Knowing that someday, it's going to be okay.

IKWUAZOM NNAMDI WENGA

Wrath of a Goddess (Nkisi)

Gun blazing, she came
Like a hunted demon
Running from calm into terror
On her trail a mountain of mud,
Softened by tears of the unwary
No root too standing to bow.
Her reign long overdue,
And her fury fettered by none.
Her flow ever determined, as though a lady scorned
She soars but beneath,
For a debt is surely owed, by those not knowing.
Her endurance waning over years.
Pity is all her wrath evokes.
Yet neglect was she stuffed with.
Her royalty trampled upon.
Her divinity turned to mockery.
Her bowels vilely suffocated.
Caged at her own home.
Her powers in mortal confrontation.
Yet we blame her for giving up,
Despite obvious alliance with karma.
She was abused and infringed upon.
Let each man prepare a feast,
For ever gaily she comes.
To feast on all in her path.
We are to blame for her vendetta.

For only but yesterday,
Did we blindly kill her tomorrow.

Life is stringent

Life is stringent to moments
Life is morning unto the stars.
Life is sunset to our struggles.
Life is the muse and fire,
The pot that cooks the lions heart.
Life is nothing but dust
Hold unto nothing in life, yet glue unto life.
Bliss in living and soulful in thought.
Is life without and with life.

(We Are Your Fathers Gone)

Out of little ant holes we emerge
Lured by chirping chicks and kola nuts
and the hypnotic spell of the drums.
For long have we slept, the seasons changing nothing,
Your libations keeping our souls moist.
May you find favor before the maker.
Come forth oh initiate, kill your fear.
For we're your fathers gone.

We bring you good tidings from the moonlight,
and blessings from the sun.
may the stars find you worthy of her glitter
years unending.
As you have nurtured us, may good fortune be your lot.
Yesterday we were men, today you're men too,
sired of the noblest of brothers.
May the iroko envy your firmness and dominion.
Be brave, for we're your fathers gone.

The axe cuts down the iroko, but yet the iroko
bears the axe.
He who has eyes should hear and may the cripple sing.
The land is evil but yet man threads upon it.
The ways of the spirits are not mere folklore
For only the pure can withstand cold in the volcano.
May the virgins honor their husbands,

and may great men find space in the legends.
Hear us now, for we're your fathers gone.

Soon we will begin the journey home.
For our kin in yonder await us.
Stay close to your tunes and neglect not your spirit.
Today seems far yet we must bow to unearth some day.
Deceive not your spirit that you are deserving of life,
for real life lies not in this life without death.
Be the men we wished to be and remember us in prayers,
for we're your fathers gone.

The Chosen Maidens

Like beautiful flowers we Bloomed
Our petals so eager to please,
Danced seductively to the melody
The cool breeze played to them.
Our skin glowed as though polished brass,
Our hips curved to perfection
Our bosoms fuller than a full moon
Our faces rival even the unknown.
With seamless flows and stamps
Upon the ground we swayed
In fluid moves only Ani could fathom
We were young and energetic
Full of steam and cherry
Even the gods knew so.
For tonight we dance and bloom
Tonight we take center stage
In preparation for the final dance
For we are the chosen ones
The finest of the land
Ani awaits us for he hosts eternally
The dance of the spirits indeed
Dance with us for tomorrow we die.

Awele

Call me Awele, the goddess of beauty
Have you seen the moon dazzle
Has the sun found such light before
Look down the river and tell me
If waters have ever been so adorable
The music sways and I salute the beings
My feet thumping the ground in splendor
Ani kisses my soles in admiration
Dance steps meant for the skies I grace
I'm Awele, daughter of tomorrow.

Beautiful Being

This beautiful being within you
Water it, nurture it
That it may bloom unsparingly.
Greatness dwells within
Guard jealously against vileness
For an era though beckons
Phoenix of the undead
Oracle of the dead
Listen to it religiously
Strain the earth to grow seeds
That the harvest you may awe at
Feed this being therefore thee mortal
For a day comes after which judgment
Alas that soul being is harvested.

Say no to Rape

She was beautiful and innocent
Her beauty wasn't her crime
Her sex wasn't also
Her dressing wasn't an excuse too
It was your lust and craving
You were just too vile
Your loins without leashes
Your soul without spirituality
Your head consumed by carnality
You forgot her pride
You adored your immorality
She cried and begged for pity
You tugged and struck for vanity
She wept her soul out -
The gods ever hearing
You had your moments of pleasure
But karma is a faithful bride
Never cheating and ever judging
Her tears will be your water
Her wails your nightmares
Her pleas will ever prick your unborn
For justice has no canal but oceans

The Salute of The Dead

We hail you, thee mortals.
From the greater side we stand
Questions of immortality have you asked
But answers have we found in sleep.
In vain to you immortalize us,
For those silver cords of bonding,
Have long been replaced by cobwebs.
Why waste your tears?
Why bother your living souls?
Let not the morgue fool you
To believe that we wander still yet.
For those dry bodies bear no hold,
And we see them not.
Rather than you mourning over debris,
Mourn over your day and still your night.
For man shall sleep one day,
A sleep beyond the shores of familiarity.
To awake on the greater side.
Then you shall see and know the truth,
If death really is the dead,
Until then, thee mortal,
Live and let live for the time dances
To music you can't afford.
We hail thee, from the greater side.

IKWUAZOM NNAMDI WENGA

We Who Died

Hello from we who died
We who lost the fight
From we who were flushed and aborted.
Greetings from the murdered
We're the drowned, fed on by the waters
We wave and hail
In happy yet sad cognition
We see you and we know you all

Can the dead hear us?

Ever wondered where they were
Ever wondered if they can hear us
If they felt our presence,
When we mourn by their graves
I wonder if death was mere sleep
If all they did was play and sing,
Telling tales of their moments
I think about my beliefs and spiritism
And I beg to know more
Do they really drink our libations
Or are we merely wasting good liquor
Do they really eat our kola nuts
Or do we just hope on threads as rope
Tell me, dear fathers long gone,
If you know the wars of today
If you remember your roles past
Do you see any hope for your sins
Rest on if it seems so
For long have we wasted tears
On graveside hills ever shallow
We shall mourn no more
Merry shall we make to names
For this life has no return
Leave that we may live

Silence

Silence is often loud and heavy
Patience ever boring and drunk.
Faith decided by some fate.
Pins fall and the ground shakes.
When did feathers add some pounds more?
Fish have grown legs on sand.
These mysteries may never end,
Until they find bearing in our phoenix.

Death was Paradise

Death was paradise
The only escape
It was bliss and cozy
It was their cocoon
And in the midst of those voices
All they saw was a path
One they swore was just
They shut the world out
Only in retaliation
For the world shut them off
By her constant insensitivity
By her self-righteousness
The world turned enemy
No one saw through the smoke screen
That they were slipping away
Into a big dark hole called depression
Slowly the hole encroached,
Only this time legally
They shut their souls forever
Because we shut our hearts at those times

**MOOD SWINGS*(the unheard shouts for help)*

These feelings have smiled knowingly yet again
Feelings long forgotten suddenly finding home
The cries of the past have again been reborn
My heart trying so hard to stay faithful
To the courage that now flees shamelessly.

This night brings with it judgment unbarred
Stripping me off of any remaining modesty
And pricking my conscience with glaring impunity
My legs wobble in guilt and my soul cracks open
As though the end has indeed come upon me.

The woes of yesterday comes gleaming wickedly
My failures beckon me to dance with them
Such mockery you can only imagine never happened
I look up to the heavens but like everything else
They unsurprisingly turn their back on me.

Remind me what faith is again?
For I have it completely in nothing but death
My only company has become the cold air
Which I'm not certain would last so long
Somehow this whole wave feels familiar.

My muse whispers a consolation from hiding
Wishing me to stay strong and fight this war
A war I don't even know when it began
I don't even know whose side I'm on
But I feel so like the enemy here.

I know this phase will pass as have others before now
But the imbalance that trails it is like no other
Turning perfect gardens into death farms in a blink
Ruining my inner peace with such ease and arrogance
I'll sleep now to wake up yesterday and skip tomorrow.

Tomorrow from yesterday

In tomorrow I saw yesterday.
So let us mourn to merry later.
For today I feel this life.
But yet tomorrow hides its face,
Infested by the throes of yesterday.
Let the harlots become classy,
Let the rogues be knighted and
Let bastards find nobility.
For what is there to fight for?
Has truth not been raped?
Or has justice not been stripped bare?
Hasn't treachery become celebrity?
The past we say was bad,
But yet tomorrow hides behind the same fate.

Life is but a Breath

Life is but a breath
Yet flight we lack in air.
Man's sight is always clouded,
By things seen from the greater side.
This thing called life varies
Nothing coming will stay rooted
For even the iroko roots will be exposed someday.
Hold then still to the fate of our faiths,
Give doubt little to feed on.
Let your inners find peace and tarry.
For in all we do and be, life is just sands away.

IKWUAZOM NNAMDI WENGA

Ogbanje

Another entry into this world
None grander than the other
I have lost count of my seasons
Sometimes, fair i come, other time brown skinned.
She would smile again today
She finally has another baby. Does she?
I look around for my unseen playmates
I giggle at their games and my mother smiles
Oh, if only she knew what tickled me
My smiles cease as I hear a familiar sound
My father approaches with the chief priest
To mark and mar my beautiful skin again?
He whispers to my father and brings out a cane
My friends scamper for they know what comes next
Chanting incantations he flogs the air
Her friends are here to disturb her again
He tells my father who shakes his head
But I have driven them away he continues
If only he knew how foolish mortals were
My mother sings in tunes of blissful hope
Maybe i might stay this time, she thinks
The priest marks me again and leaves
Chanting and warning my peers to leave me alone
I'm going to punish you all for this embarrassment
I curse under my baby nostrils.
Finally, father names me again, another funny one

I shall stay though but only to leave again
This is who I am and I must remain...

Should we all die one day

Would you be missed or rather be cursed?
Will the world still its breath for you even for a second?
Would the birds sing mourning tunes,
or will the goats go partying, bills on your stable?
or did you like to think to yourself that you're perfect?
that the world wouldn't do without you?

What would the maidens say about you?
how you broke their hearts and left them wrecked,
or how you tilled them to joyful endings.
would they wish you back even for a second,
so they could kiss you one last time?
or would they just damn you to Hades?

What would your brethren feel when your breath sleeps?
would they chant your name and sing your heroics,
or would they recount the discord you so sowed,
the lies and empty boasts you threw at them.
would they carry your corpse with disgust and spite,
or would they lift you as they would a warrior?

Your mother must miss you i guess,
but were you good to her and your conscience?
yes, she bore you and nursed you yesteryears,
but what about the times you turned down her wisdom,
just to impress some random riffraff?

your guess is now as good as mine.

What about your father? he must be pained.
a man you always felt embarrassed of in the public,
all because you met some fancy friends.
but let me ask you, who paid all through your life?
wasn't he the one? I thought you did yourself. moron,
the man wishes you would die again!

Something Called Heartbeat

The seers have gone blind
The prophets have lost the revelation
The beauty of the morning has been lost at dusk
Chaos is the new song of order
Feathers now heavy with lies
Can't you see this dawning?

The beautiful ones have been born
Yet we dwell in self-denial,
For how else do you explain the potty delusional beauty?
Man is man and woman is woman, so what?
Does that justify that unnatural craving?
I yawn in admiration of the fallen era.

Live and let live has ruined more than you think
Aren't you supposed to be my keeper?
Man has chosen life over posterity
Don't be offended by my silence over evil
That's what the system has turned saints into
Lord, how did we get here so early?

Crafty collared rogues mount the vile pulpit
Sons of Sodom seeking self-glorification from them
But can black ever become blacker? Maybe not
Canaries will never go fishing nor hens go grazing
The parrot has turned dumb in the height of the pit

HEARTBEATS BY THE RIVER

Follow the floods uphill and fish for sanity.

This era though beckons the end in beginning
Morgues rival the cold rooms in patronage
If only we listened without doubting the old ways
Shun the new song of the dead undead and maybe
Only then shall we find our heartbeat.

Stray Bullet

Shots rent the air
Ruining the quite of the evening
I drop my sponge and hurry my bath
I hear the rains too on the roof
Maybe it's just the wind tossing things

Shots yet again, this time I hear clearly
I hear my mama tell papa to come back inside
He must have wanted to see what was going on
I hear the neighbors shouting at their children
Asking them to hurry inside

Mama calls to know my whereabout
I call back to let her know I'm ok
She says for me to close the windows
That maybe it was the police shooting
Maybe after some thieves or to clear traffic

Soon we hear more shots close to the house
I hear my mama praying to all the gods to save her family
Then we hear a soul piercing scream outside
Suddenly everywhere becomes quiet and still
Maybe they're gone I say to mama

Loud wild banging on our door shock us to reality
It seems like papa's voice but now with strange chills

Mama runs and opens the door then stands still
As though she saw a ghost. She screams loud
And papa crawls into the room bleeding

I stand there transfixed like a statue
Blood everywhere on papa and mama holding him
Don't do this to me and your child please my dear
My world blanks out with all the blood and cries
My papa had been hit by a stray bullet

Will you be here

Good times are like water, everywhere,
yet the desert dwells without the luxury.
the throes of ecstasy can only last moments.
even the sun in all it's harsh splendor,
has the moon to contend with for dominance.

We've seen the good and many bad times.
you've sprinkled upon me the waters of love,
when my heart was burning with sadness.
you have nursed my damaged inner sanctum,
ever reassuring me of your undying loyalty and love.

Together we've been soil and grape alike,
producing wine only the masters of old romance
could comprehend enough to dare consume.
in you I found true peace and pristine love.
a jewel so old and yet so modern.

But will you be here when the sun sets?
will you still jump on me like a leopard?
will I still be your heart and fire?
will I still be your day and darkness as raw?
each passing day sketches winds on my garden.

But I'll be here till tomorrow and forever
loving you in ways befitting a goddess

singing you songs by the lake on our love boat
sweeping you off your feet till we pass out tired
and till breath flies away, we'll be here.

Local

You call me local because I speak my tongue.
You who is born of my very same roots.
A little hangout with foreign books and tales,
Have suddenly made you different
Now the mud seems dirty to you.
I spit on your first cries unto nature

Now your culture is just some study and thesis.
The lands that you waltzed on now sites for leisure.
Your oracles you now see as artifacts and tales,
Merely told for fun by craggy old dirty locals
How do you sleep at night? When you remember,
That those dirty fingers bathed and fed you.

I know your name and we were clan brothers.
Your ancestors were high chiefs and warriors.
Now you wear fancy robes and smoke long pipes,
And that shitting bowl you call a hat
Drink from the ovaries of nature and
See if she wouldn't have you dead

You call my food poisoning and you mock my markings.
Isn't that hypocritical of you knowing you bear same?
But let me tell you, no matter how foreign you have
Become, you remain a local to the galaxies,
And lifetimes to come unending, you are and shall
Always be a foreign local boy.

Unsure

Life is never unsure
The beauty of the snake lies in its crawl
May the rains find our seeds
Nature promises of growth without karma,
for what is love without pain

My mother sings in the ancient
of times and tales; I lust to
Her voice as though a daughter of the rivers
May she find peace and tarry long
May old age find her younger

The kingdom basks in mere folklore
Of times and men of great valor
But no matter how the chicken's wings flap,
flight it shall surely lack in the present
Gather the twigs for a fire looms

Brotherhood is the soul of mankind
Envy mocks it still yet
Arms of a brother makes or mars eternity
May the loins never break kindred spirits
And may maidens see our faiths

HEARTBEATS BY THE RIVER

I hear the drums and hail the drummer
For good soup is only as good as the maker
Warriors dance to familiar spirits and sweat
The eagle flees from great men and kings
For their caps bear a story

Childhood Memoirs

I was once like you.
I was once wild and bubbly.
I once kissed the grass, chased butterflies,
And dreamt of aliens and superheroes.

I once had a tricycle - I was still scared of falling.
I couldn't sleep with the lights on or the windows open,
For I feared monsters from my story books were real.
Mommy had to sing me to sleep.

I once had a crush on our neighbor's daughter,
I swore I was going to marry her someday.
Her hugs always made me swell like jellies.
I doubted she wasn't an angel.

My papa used to take me fishing down the lake.
I used to carry the fishing nets into the boat.
I remember papa telling me how strong I was,
And I would grin from cheek to cheek blushing.

I thought I wanted to be a doctor, but then
I thought a fire fighter was way cooler.
No," I want to be a super hero and protect you"
I would say to mama with mouthfuls of cereal.

I never liked the boy down the road,

He always called me fat and mommy's boy.
And He liked my crush too.

I could go on and on about my childhood,
But you see dear son, being young isn't all that bad.
My only regrets in life is growing up,
It takes away the bliss of childhood.

why do I write?

I was not born with a quill
I met the world bare and unknown
I had dreams like everyone else had
I wanted to shoot the stars in fortunes.

I wanted to be a lawyer, then a sailor
For I found the seas alluring
I dreamt of being a soldier, then a painter
For art and war seemed intertwined.

Then I became a teacher, imparting knowledge
Turning dull heads into brain lords with love
It came naturally, I was born into it from the stars
My contentment coming from the hopes of posterity.

All these years never for once did I forget my love
The very first of my cravings and callings
For my mind I knew was gifted with the power to create
Breathing life into words and giving souls comfort.

I write not out of boredom nor joblessness
It's beyond writing for monetary gratifications
I write not for the flattery of vain frail minds
I write for things deeper than the underworld.

I write for the very air i breathe, for my very life

I write for the universe to hear my gratitude
My ink bleeds rare divinity, something fit for eternity
Blessing the galaxy with love and sincerity of soul.

The lake that waters my heart never runs dry
For the sun gifts me light and the moon grace
My muse never departing my inner sanctums
For the stars dance to my whispers.

Poor Child Great Child

Born with no silver spoon and no golden name
A child born to poor but loving parents
Raised in poverty but with contentment
Always full of love and ever truthful
Obedient and respectful to God and nature
A child that values life and appreciates good values
Gentle as a dove but strong and confident
A poor child but a destined child indeed
One born to uplift a nation and glorify his race
Always hardworking and never pretending
A lover of culture and keeper of his faith
He shall one day rise and remain tall
For his suffering can't last forever
His determination shall one day pay off and
His honesty shall yield him good fortune
For he has understood the meaning of pain
He has felt hunger and has seen rejection
And yet his heart bears no evil nor malice
He shall rise and become the giant he was
Born and meant to be.

The Muse Behind the Poet

A thousand times you must wonder,
While sitting down and you ponder,
On what makes a poet such a wonder.
Why his poems are so good,
Why his words seem as though food.
Does he ever get tired?
Or like some device, is he wired?
You feel his every pulse,
For he writes for every cause.
You wish to know his muse,
And why his words though piercing bear no abuse.
You feel better after reading his every piece,
For it soothes your craving for deeper peace.
Is he a god?
For he wields his quill like a rod.
He gives you so much joy,
And yet he's probably just a boy.
His words must be the creator's gift,
For his delivery are always so swift.
But stress not your mind in confusion,
And embrace the realization,
That a poet is a god over his creation.
And his muse forever his inspiration.

Peace

A thousand souls lost for nothing
A thousand hearts broken forever
It's time to end the season of war
And embrace peace and forgive.

When The Earth Comes Swords Drawn

For ages have we maligned nature
Milking her to dizziness
Taking her mildness as weakness
Cutting her trees and polluting her seas.
Hunting down her forest children
We're the villains in this race
Turning the world shattered
In the wake of our greed and reckless behavior.
Now nature has had enough and has vowed revenge
By increasing the heat, drying the waters had
And by flooding us has she struck her severe blows
We're no match against her wrath
For she has endured long enough
Hoping we may change our ways
All she needed was love and appreciation,
something that this generation
has found impossible to render
But how do we appease her?
How do we soothe her pain?
Only by truly showing remorse
By planting ten trees for each fallen
By planting shrubs to beautify her skin
By stopping pollution and all
By protecting the wildlife and their habitats

By being conscious if the atmosphere
and our environment in all we do and do not do
Only when we've shown sincerity in our
repentance, shall nature turn the world for us in peace
Only then shall the climates and favor ụs.
Until then we're slaves unto our ignorance.

Street Child

Little beauty he was, cold and sad.
Left with none to care or cuddle.
The rains washing his dirty body,
the street his only family.

His eyes radiated the need for love,
a feeling the world lacks today.
Hunger is evident all over him,
his bones frail and starved

As the traffic passed by uncaring,
My conscience wouldn't let me be,
I stepped out to him and smiled,
You're going home with me today.

Mornings

The beauty of the night
Is complete with the rising of the sun
Which clears the debts of the past
While ushering in the morning
To take over the skies

Do angels really die?

The sadness still soaks many hearts
The shock still holding tight our throats
The joys and love you brought dimmed by fate
Our faces dampened by soulful deep tears
You were the oasis in the desert of poetry,
a beacon of hope for inks gone asleep
A shade for we the young and becoming.

From your pen did peace and light find words
gifting the world your all while seeking none
All you wished and craved for was the growth of arts
To see faces smile as they read beautiful words,
Words penned down from the hidden untapped hearts
You gave room for all to bond, together in purity
Couldn't darkness come much later?

Ink, pen, paper, words and people;
you brought all together to create perfection
For once, the world knew art to be the messiah,
The long lost messages of redemption to man
You were selfless and accommodating to all
Seeing each man as a vessel booming with love
You were the Gilead balm of poetry.

We shall miss you forever, dear brother and father
For in our hearts and souls do your deeds shine

your memories eternally engraved in our very existence
To your legacies do we toast our words to
For your name shall we grow stronger in unity
For you're the angel who came to humanity
But only to sooth our souls and take a bow.

****

Dedicated to the memory of a legend, late Amb KAIRAT DUISSENOV PARMAN, founder and immediate past Chairperson of the WORLD NATIONS WRITERS UNION.

Lonely moments

The sadness this night is heavy,
For I have never felt so alone.
I feel as though drowning under,
With no one to rescue me yet.
The darkness doesn't help much,
For I see shadows everywhere.
The moon seems to play along,
denying my tears light to glow.
I feel the indifference of time,
for the clock had lost it's tick.
She isn't here tonight to sing,
to tuck me into bed with songs,
This night will surely tarry long,
Because my mother isn't here.
I have never felt so lonely.

"Golden whispers"

These words bounce in my heart
Seeking outlet in my gaze
The feelings i fight so hard
Still find their way into my head
The madness of the world is cunny
With fate pitting us against faith
I find this phase bemusing and
I know I'm not alone in thought
But yet I have learned from trying
Just so hard to voice out my pain
I have lost count of my tears and
My days of seeming light against
The nights now ever so dim
I shall speak no more audible
Words but in my silence shall
My whispers shatter the darkness
For in this silence have i found peace.

Human Goods

The story we may never forget
but yet we pray never happens again.
Tales of our fathers gone and old,
Bound in chains and rope like goats,
Shackled and collared like stray dogs.
Whips dancing on frail backs all,
Limbs failing and bones cracking
Humans herded as though cattle
Made to walk miles unending while the
slave owners ride on horse backs
Nothing can explain nor atone for the hurt
the pains and lost bloodlines,
But in the desert of hopelessness,
an oasis of hope always surfaces;
In the spirits unbroken and faithful,
Not to any being but to time and endurance
But though the trade of flesh may have
Been abolished, the wounds are still sour
the offended still hunted and the predators
Unyielding The old trade taking new forms
and ever cleansing not the past but
rather imbibing hatred and bitterness
into our very hearts. We're one today,
we're one tomorrow and the divide of colors
Have no hold we should break the bonds
Of modern slavery and reject racism in all its forms.
The world needs more humans than colors.

Spring time.

The smell of fresh flowers
And dew caress my deepest senses.
I'm alive in nature once again
Butterflies dance over my head in
Perfect symphony and I marvel
The pains of dryness and emptiness
washed away and life is reborn again
But there's more to spring than blooming
Nature and rebirth spring remind us of life itself
That though all may seem lost,
There's always a time for stability
As those pretty flowers grow again
So, shall we smile and grow also
For even in our darkest moments,
There must come spring time.

Lonely corner

Some days seem just not familiar
I wonder if the stars are at war
or if my thoughts are merely solo
I just can't find answers.

A sweet sound warms my sad ears
I look towards the sound and there they were
A kid and his kitty cat
He played his flute to her seen joy.

For a moment I saw innocence pure
I felt ashamed of my worried mind
If he could be this happy with just his cat, why
shouldn't I be...

hard work pays

Life's struggles seem without end
The troubles of life always vicious
Vanity stares into my face,
As if to mock my hard work.
A clean living in a corrupt world
like ours isn't so easy
Corruption rules the day and
Good people soon lose the will of honesty
But i must persevere and work harder,
for dreams of a better tomorrow do I have
I know my sweat would pay off
I know that truth always wins
I lift my head high knowing that
Someday my efforts and dreams will be accomplished.

******Because I am a woman******

For creations from forever
Have I been looked over
Cast to stay behind without
As little as much as a voice
Barred even by religion from reaching the skies
Not even the stars spare me the torture
For they deny me their shine on my darkest days
I'm seen as weak and vulnerable, a mere afterthought
My words and counsel do you cast away in derision
I stoop and squat to answer unto nature's calls
How does that make me any weaker?
The sins of the angels do I bear and
For the blindness at soul of the early one do I suffer
Yes I ate the forbidden, but so did he too
My fingers toil and my heart broken into pieces
But yet still I love without restraints
For my soul looms not in sorrow but over
The bliss of a forgiving mother
The world though an ungrateful child, still the
Love passed from my bosom never withers
In my darkest of lights do I still give light
To your fights and music to your souls
I'll still tend to your wounds and pleasures alike
Warming you up on cold nights
I carry the world and mankind undivided
I am untamable and bound for the vain stars

My reign will never be cut off and my soul
Will forever remain faithful to my cause and fire
For I'm a woman and I'm god.

****Songs of hypocrisy****

A smile so broad it overshadowed the sun
Lies so sweet they rivaled honey combs
Promises so alluring that the angels melted
Dirty babies and saggy breasted women
Selling their futures with inspiring ease and craftiness

The masses have long lost hope
The table long losing balance
The fires of patriotism quenched by legal illegality
Camouflaged as law enforcement agencies
Opposition exists only on the media
And when they try getting serious
The exterminators come in with terror reigns
All this fallacy all just for power
And because a people and generation
Are yet to speak up in oneness and fire
And until then I tell you
These songs of hypocrisy shall last a day more.

****Resilience comes from within****

We're more than the trials we face
For in our struggles do we find hope
Holding unto nothing but the will to survive
Our inner sanctum feeding our spirits and
Our souls sprouting roots into perseverance

We're hurt and bitter, yes
But our hearts know no hate no evil
For unto each day do we pray to live
Our energy tapped from inner peace
Fueling our fires with logs of our pain

Our hearts may be scared to hope, or believe
But trust me, even our fears have hope
For they believe we're weaker and vulnerable
Why do we cry when we hurt?
Tell me to wipe our eyes in fluidity

Can the maker hear our supplications?
Can he feel our pain and grief?
Or are our depressed minds too dirty?
Too dipped in pain and fear for him to soil his hands?
We're sorry if we lack faith, but truth seems not far away

In our lonely moments
When our hearts know no anchor

HEARTBEATS BY THE RIVER

In the waters of frustration and hopelessness
Who do we run to? How do we even run?
For we have lost our feet long ago

The rope or a jump? Maybe even a drink of bliss
Would put our pain away forever
Our souls cuddled by assuring demons
Who have come to be the only family
Tell us, if life isn't just beautiful

But we're alive still for another morning
Awaiting the blooming flowers
Feeling the early dews on our fingers
We shall continue the story called life
For in our voices within lies resilience

*****

(This poem is dedicated to us all who go through all forms of pain and struggle)

*****Golden Tango*****

In a lonely dark corner
My mind filled with buzzing air
Deep strings struggling for a peek outside my soul
The voices getting ever clearer but cold

I feel the muse but lack the words
My heart beats rapidly like old war drums
I must be losing my sanity
Demons tearing at my insanity

I grab some sheets and my gaze finds a pen
The feelings ever clearer now becoming voices
Voices standing as though iroko trees
Waiting to be axed unto my paper

Now I see my words and smile knowingly
My burden becoming lighter and easy
I scribble out my anger, love and confusion
Giving feathers to whispers

Now you see and read my wordy fires
You breath my inspirations and chant my soul
But moments ago, they were just echoes from my muse
Now joined by pen and paper in a golden tango.

rare

On countless nights drunk I returned
Clawing through the dark night
Like a knowing wolf seeking scent
Tearing down an open door
In stupid feats of anger and insanity

Words unholy have I muttered and flung
Feeling so full of myself but still empty
Seeing my foolishness as manhood
Soaking my spirit in spirits still yet
Silly wise fool indeed

Overcome by anger have I hit you
Scaring and tearing your flawless skin
Leaving your heart bleeding and worn out
Your soul praying for His touch upon me
My ego meanwhile basking in vain superiority

Whores have I soiled our bed with
Concubines do I find company amongst
Romping and thrusting into vile holes
When you're out there cold in the dark
How foolish can my loins be

Yet pray is all you do for me
Tearing the heavens down in teary prayers

Stripping Him almost bare in your desperate pleas
That he touch my soul even just for a day
So that I may find my path

You know the times must change
So you relent not a bit
Clinging unto His words despite my blasphemies
And my boasts of needing not His salvation
After all He Himself was killed

But yet you still stand strong
And despite all I do and say
You never told me off to Hades
Your soul has always loved me still
And smiled down in my sleep.

#A woman is easy to find, but a good woman is rare. Dedicated to all women who despite the pains, emotional and mental torture they go through, still find it in their hearts to pray for, care and love their man.

solace

Reach out to me
On those soul crowdy nights
And show me the light I need
Without making me feel indebted
To the rhythm of peace

woes of war

Bloodthirsty dictators, unholy leaders.
Chests full of nothing but pride and arrogance.
Souls lacking of human elements,
hearts devoid of love and light, bitter to stupor.
Commands given for destruction and mayhem,
Boys, men and fathers all bonded by arms,
All bound to die in living to kill fellow brethren.

Splattered limbs and charred flesh adorn the grounds.
Headless bodies litter like pawns on a chess board.
Vultures glorify the soulless skies joyously.
Even the wind seems to concur with the anguish,
Denying the air around freshness.
This is all simply catastrophe and damnation.
How did we get so heartless?

Shouts, cries, wails and piercing screams fill the air,
Smoke dancing up towards the teary skies.
Fathers killing fathers and sons alike.
Women turned widows on sunny sunless days
and children becoming fatherless on starless nights.
The chaos ever unending and draining,
Filling the belly of the earth to stupendous fullness.

Little children crying in hunger and fear,
Their mothers turning harlots to feed and survive.

The overlords have become the darkness at sunrise,
their hold and tentacles covering even the moon.
Terror is the order of the day as the system collapses.
Peace has fled never to return but replaced by hate,
How can life get so bad?

Senseless wars caused by nothing but sheer ego, pride
And fool hardiness of unrepentant tyrants camouflaged
In human skins. Now we suffer over their fantasies.
We're made to understand the harsh realities of life.
Enemies and death are now the guardian words of watch.
Trust has become history and hope a lost dream.
How did we get into this?

But we are alive to tell this story,
Alive even if only for today's sadness.
These wars have rendered us homeless and empty,
But it has made us appreciate each passing second
and breath.
Awaiting the next airstrikes or the gun bouts that
embrace us.
Our spirits loitering the earth in vain mortality
as we await
Death but still yet praying to survive a day more.

****Dare not touch, she's only a baby****

She's only four, a baby
yet your loins rise to lust.
She's only crawling, a baby
yet you touch her as though a toy.
her mama trusted you to watch her,
her papa saw you as kin and blood
yet all you had in mind was carnality.
And like a wolf you devoured an innocent baby,
tearing her up like she was but rags,
pleasing your shameful self and ruining a poor baby.
How cursed can you be and how damned is your soul?
This evil continues, each time getting more intense.
Now she's seven, fully adapted to your sins and evil,
bent into loving your every touch, looking forward to
your visits even and telling her baby mind she loves you.
you've made her a little nymph fairy, for she lacks
control now,
her mama still oblivious and her papa still your brother.
Every night, you invade her sanity, purity and pride,
each session taking along a piece of her future and soul.
Now she's grown and fourteen, she can't bear to
see you go,
she has become the curse you so desired, a plaything.

She can't stand the sight of other but she craves
your touch!
I spit on you and your unborn generations!
For you have ruined an innocent baby and turned
her whoring.
Raping her gradually into sinful cooperation and
endurance,
teaching her the forbidden, ruining her pride and joy.
Now her mama begins to notice her withdrawn attitude
around others but you, she thinks you're just her fa-
vorite uncle.
How wrong could she be? Trusting a pedo like you.
A child is a child and never a sexual object.
I pray she finds the voice to speak out someday, I pray.
I pray she gets all the help she can get and get it early too.
As for you, the cosmos owe you pain and denial of peace.
For your kind are the curses that mankind are
plagued with.

(Rape of minors/babies, have always been one aspect of sexual abuse/harassment that we overlook. Over a million babies are daily violated by adults and we do nothing about it. This cannot continue and I say we start now to fight this hydra headed monster. Rape in all forms, is evil!)

****Dear God****

I come begging again today
not for riches or wealth
but for the gifts so precious yet that we lack
I come seeking that you take a look down and see
if this is what you really wanted as your children;
If they're really your true image.

I come begging for the sickly ones
For the dying bones and frayed limbs
Soothe their pain and make them whole
Or is it too much to ask?
Are their sins that much to forgive?
Prove my doubting mind wrong.

I pray for the abused children and women
Who have been put through hell alive
I pray for those who died from the pains of rape
Didn't you hear their cries as they struggled?
You were the only name they thought would help out
Let not their villains go without everlasting hell.

I pray for India and her children
For too long have they experienced living hell
Deaths and sickness everywhere as though sands
Don't they deserve your mercies too?
Are they not also your children and creations?

Take away this scary dawn from their souls I beg.

I pray for the widows who have lost him but not you
You promised them marriage forevermore
I hold your words in the book as witness
Yet you watch them mistreated by a raging society
You can bear seeing them accused and slandered?
Where's the love you promised them?

I pray for Nigeria my country
Once giants but now cannibalistic to her children
Her system and leaders devouring hopes and dreams
armed bandits and herders slaughtering whatever is left
Death has become the reigning news and song
War chants heard so closely and hunger ever dominant.

I pray and plead for Africa
That her ages of hurt and neglect be seen to
For long has she been scorned and scandalized colorfully
by the world she has forever mothered and nurtured
May she be seen as equal in the tongues of men
For she's as important as the blood in their veins.

I plead for the lost brethren over beyond
Shut and gunned down by racism in official clothes
Murdered for being colored by their supposed protectors
May their blood not dry in the sands of vengeance
May their cries be the torment to their oppressors
May their memories never be forgotten.

I pray for the climate and nature
May they show us not the hate we have shown them
May the trees forgive and may the waters not wash us off
For generations have we plundered nature and
left her bare
I know her vengeance is deserving but please Lord
Heal her wounds that she may spare.

I pray for my brethren in soul and mind
Those gifted with the magic of creativity
Penning down words worthy of eternity
Bless their souls with love, light and peace
For through their ink have many found consolation
In their veins are wisdom embodied to live forever.

For the depressed I pray comfort
Hold them closer to feel your love and judge them not
For the world has shut its doors on them
And turned deaf ears to their gloomy cries
Melt their pain away and sow in happiness
Now is the time to prove your fatherly love and care.

For the world I pray and plead
That we may see war for the evil it is and shun it
That we may embrace and always seek peace
That we may always carry each other in our days
And love at night without color sentiments and race
For we're all we have and would ever have.

I pray not for my heartbeat and inner peace

But for your glory to erode all the impurities
and reset the world to peaceful nights and glorious mornings
I know you are more than capable to do more
But this little is all I ask and pray for
Until then my heart is broken seeking life and air.

***** *War & Sunrise* **

Gunshots, cannon shots and bombs
Bullets, blood, splattered limbs and smoke
Bandages, slings, stretchers and sirens
Soldiers shouting over their lungs
Commanders issuing damning orders
Death showing obvious dedication
The madness continues like an orchestra

How did we get here?
When did brothers turn to killers?
Forgetting thoughts of paradise and peace
Wearing envy, bitterness and demons
Their hearts replaced with rocks
And their souls possessed by hades
Becoming tools for under lord

How can the fate of nations and lives
Mean nothing to egoistic lords and leaders
Sending innocent civilians mourning
And turning patriotic soldiers into assassins
Who gun down weeping mothers, babes and men
How can these beasts have peace and sleep?
When the earth cries of full stomach, of flesh

Can the heavens hear the cries of the widows
Who lost caring fathers to the unforgiving bullet

HEARTBEATS BY THE RIVER

Do the stars feel no shame shining on bloody nights
I curse the sun for brightening the days of murderers
The air betrays me by blessing the lungs of beasts
I know the maker owes me apologies forever
For gifting life to unworthy sons of sin

Life has lost its flavor and fluidity
But yet hope abounds
For in those gleamy eyes of orphaned children
I see glitters of sunrise
A generation coming back to the beginning
Where all we had was naked untamed love
For all humanity and beyond the cosmos

A time is coming when the voices of change
Enjoined by the dreams of redemption
Shall rebuild the bridges burnt by the past
Armed this time with peace, dialogue and trust
And love for all mankind undivided
I see and seek this new dawn of sunrise
For what is life without life and love

So the time is now or never
We must preach the message of forgiveness
For revenge is how we even got into this mess
A kiss and a flower for an eye
Spreading the gospel of oneness and respect
Hold my hands in brotherhood and communion
As we redeem our glory and walk into our era.

(Reasons to live)

On dark days when the sun is banished
and the moon finds joy in my darkness,
I bask in the unknown wonder of nothingness.
I have lived here and still up here in my head.
I've seen true friends go by and hatred growing over.
I've felt the coldness of death and tasted denials.
Why do we live, I've asked myself inclusive of you.
If it's to go in and multiply like the holy book says,
then we've done more than just enough and more,
for the world now is full of people but without people.

Why then do I live?

For the birds that fly over my head without judgment,
gifting me solace by their consoling melodies.
Early morning dances as they perch and peck by
my window,
always leave me hoping for better joys within my heart.
They have become my reason to await the morning air.

For the trees in the forests.
Trees that we have abused and neglected.
Running my fingers across them makes me gasp
in wonder,
for how can something so dormant be more un-
derstanding,
enduring and more forgiving than humans who hurt it.
Giving then shelter and shade still on thunderous nights.

For the flowers that brighten my soul with colors and
fragrance.
Always assuring me of beauty in every down moment.
Adorning my world with nothing but pristine confluence
of harmony and peace. Defying the hate of the world.

For the loving animals that understand without doubt.
Forgiving each scar and embracing my flaws in loving.
They're the better versions of humanity.
For they hold and remember no grudge.

For the waters that dampen my heat and wet my tongue.
You've been the earliest of nature and her most faithful offspring.
Washing my sins and impurities alike, without a frown.
Watering the ungrateful world and blessing mother earth.

I live not for the things of this sinful world.
I have felt nothing but envy, greed, war, rejection, pain, regrets, judgment and nothing holding in this sphere.
most often than never have i wondered and even dreamed about the peace of life on the other side.

But yet i still strive to live,
For even in the midst of our certain imperfections,
I still find souls worthy of connection, cursed to pain as i am.
In them do I find redemption and cause.
For we're all slaves unto a soulless era.
Together we breath and claw our way through limitations, obstacles and self-imposed coma.

I live because we live, because the universe lives
and because nature promises to love and care forever,
Without pretense or expectations.

we're one.

The sun brightens all humans,
Notwithstanding their colors.
The moon and stars gift their glow,
Without a care about race or tribe.
The seas quench the thirsts of all,
Without a worry about faith or gods
Why can't we humans love too?
Why must religion, race and color
Be the cause of unrest and hate?
We must learn to live in peace,
For we're all the same blood.
Our tongues may be different,
But we breathe the same air,
Live on the same earth and
When dead we all turn dust.
We must all unite in endurance,
Unity, love and peace.
For only by peaceful coexistence,
Shall we know true love and peace.

**There shall be a Season **

The blue oceans rise to my joy
Sending my heart on a joyous voyage
The smell of fresh flowers ever alluring
I honestly pray they're roses
For what is life without thorns
The stars in perfect chemistry, gift me a dance
Holding hands with the sun, in convoy with the moon

My heart finds my soul amazing
For my mind whispers love to my steps
This gift of life though undeserving
Do i cherish with beautiful bonds in peace
For long in dark ages have i lost light
Seeing the world as but without soul
Never worthy of even a cuddle

Now this mornings are here, ever brighter still
My gardens in abundance of colors
And my cheeks overfed with blushes
My heart leaps joyfully at my laughter
This lamp has been lit and hung
For the world to find glow and muse
May this season be without end.

What The World Needs

The world today is bleeding and dying.
Mankind ever becoming close to extinction.
Nature getting so close to her tipping point.
The seasons of self destruction are upon us.

The world today needs peace and tolerance.
From Gaza down to Nigeria, the genocides must end.
Else the world will be littered with bitter children
turned orphans.
We must end all senseless wars and choose peace.

The world today must purge itself of racism and tribalism.
We must also not choose religion over peaceful
coexistence.
For we're all of one creation and must return to
dust someday.
No one is holier and no one can claim the right true path.

The world today must embrace nature and seek
redemption.
For long have we murdered an innocent universe.
We must correct our environmental mistakes
and damages.
Wildlife and forestry must be respected and protected.

The world today should show love for humanity.

For what are we without one another, nothing.
We must respect life and try to sow seeds of happiness.
Genuine charity should overwhelm our hearts and lives.

We must realize that all we have is just us.
Nature bore us all and has always played mother role.
We must start now on this morning of redemption.
May our hearts find the peace, light and love it craves.

We were once humans

once upon a time in some fairy garden,
Our origins by faith took off,
Setting the pace for the world today.
Stories of forbidden fruits were we all taught,
Made to see the serpent as evil.
Never taking blame for our undoing.

Rapidly we grew and further encroached the earth,
Bringing with us destruction and recklessness.
Plundering nature to stupendous starvation of warmth.
Cutting down trees and hunting creatures into extinction.
We never for once saw our actions as wrong.
Murderers did we become unto our roots.

Our vain quest for powers leading to many senseless wars.
Forcefully feeding the earth with explosions and death.
Flooding the waters with blood and killing the poor
aqua lives.
Nothing was spared on our trails of destruction.
The menace becoming worse by the minute.
We forgot about the sanity of the environment.

Then came the science and tech ages.
Innocent animal lives wasted in inhuman labs and tests.
Nature losing more grounds each passing day.
Death seducing weapons produced on the rapid,

Nations threatening peace armed with nuclear weapons.
The world becoming one hell of a test pad for death.

The ecosystem losing balance on the steady.
The forests losing her trees, shrubs, beings and essence.
Chaos becoming the new world order and anthem.
Soulless laws passed and infant annihilation endorsed.
Sins of holy Gomorrah finding stronger alliance and
acceptance.
Racism and tribalism finding the keys to our hearts.

We're all of one creation yet we're divided by our
own creation.
Suicides ruling the minds of the depressed brethren,
All because nobody cared to lend an ear or kindness.
Corruption and unholy riches paying for our conscience.
Our relationship with the heavens becoming ever severed,
Not by blades but by our ignorance and pride in vanity.

Now the climates are changing to our utter bewilderment.
How can we feign ignorance and play the victim card?
Aren't we just self deceitful and petty?
Can we deny our role in extinguishing nature?
What was nature's offence or crime?
Nothing, yet we drained her of life and serenity.

The waters now drown us amidst our tears and cries.
The very air we so polluted and desecrated now
choking us.
The grounds caving us in, the trees denying us moist airs.

But who are we to blame when all we did was
abuse nature.
We're shadows of what humanity was and should be.
And now we're at the mercy of our creations.
Pity far gone.

We were once humans; soft and pure.
But now we must bear the brunt and feel our poisons.
A world that cared and provided for us now rises in
damnation.
Where do we run to and why should we even
plead mercy.
Shouldn't we remain the arrogant breed that we've been?
We lost our survival the moment we lost our humanity.

(Climate change is real. Let's plant trees, stop pollution, genocide, testing of experiments on animals and let's embrace peace, oneness and love. Nature has risen from slumber. We're all we have.)

Where do warriors sleep? (Tribute to a loving father)

My hands still shake and my fingers wobble woe fully.
The reality still not having sunk in completely.
Your voice I still hear and your words echoing so close.
My feet dragging on without reason to walk anymore.
Under your wings did I explore this hostile world,
Your watchful eyes ever roaming around me.

In your glory did my morning sun find light.
From your unending wisdom did my mind find support.
The memories of your laughter sends shivers
down my spine.
How can I convince my senses and inner sanctums that
you're gone?
When all you radiated was life, contentment and
discipline.
Who do I hold now when the storms gather in coup?

What were you even?
A father, brother, mentor, guardian or a demigod?
All those days dragging into months that you were stone
cold asleep,
My soul wished to hear your idolized voice, to see
your glory.

Touching your cold body was the hardest thing i found
myself doing.
Oh, did I not pray just about everyday to every being
holy, I did.

The world feels quiet without you.
The gods now starve of your dedication and homage.
The long morning and evening walks now forgotten.
Did you know that even the dog slept on with
you that day?
How else do you describe the feeling of darkness?
Falling stars dragging the sun down upon the moon.

Your legacies and values do I now cling to.
For in your dusk has my morning found reason to rise.
Your love for justice and equity has no mortal rival.
A kiss for an eye was your philosophy, a dedicated
truth seeker.
The world may never know the soft part of you, but I
gratefully do.
You're the oasis in the desert of this morning called life.

A song for you each passing day; that you may find peace.
I know the cosmos know your worth and the maker
your faith.
My consolation lies in your words imprinted on my heart.
Be good to nature and life, you would always advised.
I still hold the doctrines of the rose close to my soul.
But tell me, father, where do warriors sleep?

In memory of the late Chief Engr B. O. P. Adibuah, CP wrks rtd. (The Ajie ukadiugwu of Onitsha) 1/9/1942 - 2/7/2020. Rest in power!

**lost faiths*

My fathers were the originals.
They saw the world for what it was.
They communed with their ancestors.
They revered the spirits of the dead.
Building bonds stronger than life itself.
My fathers had name for all the stars, even for the moon.
The sun was worshipped and revered.
Early morning incantations were offered
to please their ancestors, spirits and gods.
They believed in unity and devotion.
Everything had a reason and a place in their destiny.
Each child born was named according to his sup-
posed stars.
But now we've lost touch with our past.
All in the search for civilization.
My generation has derailed from the roots
Of our very existence.
We have lost the faith to fate.
A lost faith indeed.

Acknowledgements

Putting together a poem, not to talk of a whole book, is the most daunting of tasks. Most people like to think that poetry is as easy as nursery rhymes. But then that is not usually the case. In the many months of my working to put up this beautiful work, I was never alone for a second. It may have taken just me to write the book, yes, but it took a whole lot of support, encouragement and motivation from so many people for me to achieve this feat.

In no particular order I'd love to thank these amazing people who believed in my passion. I'll start from my mother. She's the reason I'm here in the first place. She's also the reason this book is here today. Thank you, mom for loving me despite my many shortcomings.

To the lady who chose the title for this book, Ofodueze Adaeze Cherry (Nwunye Nwoke Anambra), thank you for buying into my dream. Samuella Conteh, my godmother from far away Sierra Leone, I say a big thank you for not only supporting me but also for writing the forward to this book. I'm humbled that a global figure as you would find me worthy. Robert Gillette, my ever-supporting mentor all the way from the USA, thank you for promoting and always encouraging me. To the Motivational Strips family, I say a big thank you for giving not just me but many upcoming poets the spotlight to show our abilities. To Samuel

Cavero and AEADO, thank you for promoting and honoring me. Chinwe Ebo and Iveanyi Nezianya, thanks for being amazing babies, our bonding was never by chance but by fate and our love has no rival. A big thank you to pious Okaneme for his honest reviews. To Nwando Ogbuotobo, my jewel from Anike, you're the muse behind my smiles and the water that wets my soul. Thank you for not giving up. To miracle Nzubechi, you're loved beyond words. To the Nzegwu family, thank you for buying into my dream and for pushing my works with so much passion and love. You guys are the perfect example of love, unity and family. To the Kulture Magazine family, you guys are the best. To the Onitsha Literary Society (Oliona), I say we keep going higher in our efforts to achieve the society of our dreams. To my best friend, sister, mother and daughter, Onyinye Sylvia Diana Mozie, I say thank you for giving me the best moments of my life and for showing me what true love and friendship means. To the LA Familia, thank you for giving me the best orientation as a gentleman and rose bearer.

And to everyone who has shown support in numerous ways, I say thank you to you all. May we all live to excel.

www.ingramcontent.com/pod-product-compliance
Lightning Source LLC
LaVergne TN
LVHW050959080826
845145LV00009B/2363

* 9 7 8 1 0 0 5 5 0 5 7 0 7 *